He has constrained ...

— He has excited domestic injur... ...

...d destruction of all ages, sexes and conditions. ...

...d injury. A Prince, whose character is thus marked by every act which ...

here. We have warned them from time to time of attempts by their legislature to extend an un... ...them/

...n. We have appealed to their native justice and magnanimity, and we hav... ...

our connections and correspondence. They too have been deaf to the voice ...

...d hold them, as we hold the rest of mankind, Enemies in War, in Peace Fr... ...

...al Congress, Assembled, appealing to the Supreme Judge of the world for ... ...

...nection between them and the State of Great Britain, is and ought to be Free an... ...

...ct Alliances, establish Commerce, and to do all other Acts and Things which Independent ...

...nce on the Protection of divine Providence, we mutually pledge to each other our Lives, our Fortunes ...

Josiah Bartlett
Wm Whipple
Sam Adams
John Adams
Rob Treat Paine
Elbridge Gerry
Step Hopkins
William Ellery
Roger Sherman
Sam Huntington
Wm Williams
Oliver Wolcott
Matthew Thornton

Hancock

Rob Morris
Benjamin Rush
Benj. Franklin
John Morton
Geo Clymer
Ja Smith
Geo Taylor
James Wilson
Geo Ross
Casar Rodney
Geo Read
Tho M Kean

Wm Floyd
Phil. Livingston
Fran Lewis
Lewis Morris

Rich Stockton
Jno Witherspoon
Fra Hopkinson
John Hart
Abra Clark

...ase
...re
...ll of Carrollton

...ge Wythe
...d Henry Lee
...efferson
...Harrison
...Nelson jr.
...Lightfoot Lee
...r Braxton

*Our Lives
Our Fortunes
Our Sacred Honor*

Our Lives
Our Fortunes
Our Sacred Honor

Paul Harvey

WORD BOOKS, PUBLISHER

Waco, Texas

Printed in the United States of America
Library of Congress catalog card number: 75-24827

Designed and hand lettered by Dennis Hill

Preface

The how and why of our beloved Republic are so much better known and understood than the "who."

The United States of America was born in 1776. But it was conceived 169 years before that.

The earliest settlers had watered the New World with much sweat, had built substantial holdings for themselves and their families. When the time came to separate themselves from a tyranny an ocean away, at best it meant starting all over again after the ravages of war.

Researching what you are about to read gave a new dimension to my reverence for our nation's first citizens.

All others of the world's revolutions before and since were initiated by men who had nothing to lose.

Our founders had everything to lose... nothing to gain... except one thing.......

Our Lives
Our Fortunes
Our Sacred Honor

You remember the cherry tree story
a long time after you forget the more
earth-shaking, history-making episodes
in the life of George Washington.

You've misplaced in your memory the
details of Ben Franklin's statesmanship,
but you remember his flying a kite.

Joyce Kilmer was a great military hero,
but the only thing you personally recall
about him... is his poetic tribute to trees.

*M*aybe of this current decade, that which will be best remembered will not be its wars and its moon rockets or its giants who lived and died. Maybe all that will survive to linger in the day-by-day vocabulary of generations yet unborn... will be a song about a Tennessee frontiersman or the incident at the window that night a speck of dust blew in and penicillin was discovered.

But for any eve of the Fourth of July,
I, Paul Harvey, do bequeath unto you
something to remember.

You may not be able to quote one line from the Declaration of Independence at this moment; henceforth, you will always be able to quote at least one line.

It's in the last paragraph where you will recall, when I remind you, it says, "We mutually pledge to each other our Lives, our Fortunes, and our sacred Honor."

You recognize those impressive words, but you don't understand them until you know THE REST OF THE STORY.

In the Pennsylvania State House, that's
now called Independence Hall in Philadelphia,
the best men from each of the colonies
sat down together. It was a fortunate hour
in our nation's history, one of those rare
occasions in the lives of men when we
had greatness to spare.

These were men of means, well educated.
Twenty-four were lawyers and jurists. Nine
were farmers and owners of large
plantations.

On June 11 a committee sat down to draw up a declaration of independence. We were going to tell our British fatherland, no more rule by redcoats! Below the dam of ruthless foreign rule, the stream of freedom was running shallow and muddy. We were lighting the fuse to dynamite that dam.

This pact, as Burke later put it, "was a partnership between the living and the dead and the yet unborn." There was no bigotry, no demagoguery in this group. All had shared hardships.

Jefferson finished a draft of the document in seventeen days. Congress adopted it in July. So much is familiar history.

Now...

King George III had denounced all rebels in America as traitors. Punishment for treason was hanging.

The names now so familiar to you from the several signatures on that Declaration of Independence ... the names were kept secret for six months. For each knew the full meaning of that magnificent last paragraph ... in which his signature pledged his life, his fortune and his sacred honor.

Fifty-six men placed their names beneath that pledge. Fifty-six men knew — when they signed — that they were risking everything.

They knew if they won this fight, the best they could expect would be years of hardship in a struggling nation. If they lost, they'd face a hangman's rope.

But they signed... the pledge.

And they did, indeed, pay the price. That is THE REST OF THE STORY.

Here is the documented fate of that gallant fifty-six.

Carter Braxton

Thomas Lynch Junr.

Tho M. Kean

Carter Braxton of Virginia, wealthy planter
and trader, saw his ships swept from the
seas. To pay his debts he lost his home
and all his properties and died in rags.

Thomas Lynch, Jr, who signed that pledge
was a third-generation rice-grower. Aristocrat.
Large plantation owner. After he signed,
his health failed. With his wife he set out
for France to regain his failing health.
Their ship never got to France, was never
heard from again.

Thomas McKean of Delaware was so
harassed by the enemy that he was forced
to move his family five times in five months.
He served in Congress without pay, his
family in poverty and in hiding.

*V*andals looted the properties of Ellery and Clymer and Hall and Gwinnett and Walton and Heyward and Rutledge and Middleton.

And Thomas Nelson, Jr., of Virginia, raised two million dollars on his own signature to provision our allies ... the French fleet. After the war he personally paid back the loans, wiped out his entire estate. He was never reimbursed by his government.

In the final battle for Yorktown he, Nelson, urged General Washington to fire on his ... Nelson's ... own home, which was occupied by Cornwallis.

It was destroyed. He died bankrupt and was buried in an unmarked grave. Thomas Nelson, Jr., had pledged "his life, his fortune, and his sacred honor."

William Ellery

Geo Clymer

Lyman Hall

Button Gwinnett

Geo Walton

Thos Heyward Junr.

Edward Rutledge /.

Arthur Middleton

Thos Nelson ji.

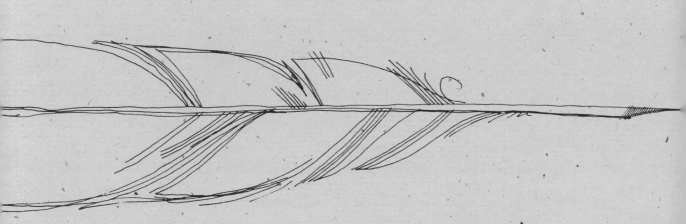

Fras. Hopkinson

Fran. Lewis

Rich. Stockton

Thos. Heyward Junr.

The Hessians seized the home of Francis Hopkinson of New Jersey.

Francis Lewis had his home and everything destroyed, his wife imprisoned. She died within a few months.

Richard Stockton, who signed that Declaration, was captured and mistreated and his health broken to the extent that he died at fifty-one. His estate was pillaged.

Thomas Heyward, Jr., was captured when Charleston fell.

John Hart was driven from his wife's bedside while she was dying. Their thirteen children fled in all directions for their lives. His fields and gristmill were laid waste. For more than a year he lived in forests and caves and returned home after the war to find his wife dead, his children gone, his properties gone; he died a few weeks later of exhaustion and a broken heart.

Lewis Morris saw his land destroyed, his family scattered.

Philip Livingston died within a few months from the hardships of the war.

John Hart

Lewis Morris

Phil. Livingston

John Hancock

John Hancock history remembers best due to a quirk of fate rather than anything he stood for. That great, sweeping signature attesting to his vanity towers over the others. One of the wealthiest men in New England, he stood outside Boston one terrible night of the war and said, "Burn Boston, though it makes John Hancock a beggar, if the public good requires it."

He, too, lived up to the pledge.

*O*f the fifty-six, few were long to survive.

Five were captured by the British and tortured before they died. Twelve had their homes... from Rhode Island to Charleston ... sacked, looted, occupied by the enemy, or burned. Two lost their sons in the army. One had two sons captured. Nine of the fifty-six died in the war, from its hardships or from its more merciful bullets.

I don't know what impression you had of the men who met that hot summer in Philadelphia. But I think it is important that we remember this about them.

They were not poor men or wild-eyed pirates. They were men of means. Rich men, most of them, who enjoyed much ease and luxury in their personal living.

*N*ot hungry men. Prosperous men. Wealthy landowners, substantially secure in their prosperity.

But they considered liberty — and this is as much as *I* shall say of it — they had learned that liberty — is so much more important than security — that they pledged their lives... their fortunes... and their sacred honor.

And they fulfilled their pledge.

They paid the price.

*A*nd freedom was born.

The Declaration of Independence, July 4, 1776: "For the support of this Declaration, with a firm reliance on the protection of Divine Providence, we mutually pledge to each other our Lives, our Fortunes, and our sacred Honor."

Paul Harvey